ABSTRACT EXPRESSIONISM

Richard Spilsbury

Heinemann Library
Chicago, Illinois

Customer service 888-454-2279
Visit our website at www.heinemannraintree.com

 Produced for Heinemann Library by
White-Thomson Publishing Ltd
Bridgewater Business Centre
210 High Street, Lewes
East Sussex BN7 2NH, U.K.

Edited by Ruth Nason and Megan Cotugno
Designed by Mayer Media Ltd
Picture research by Amy Sparks and Ruth Nason
Originated by Chroma Graphics
Printed and bound in China by Leo Paper Products

13 12 11 10 09
10 9 8 7 6 5 4 3 2

Library of Congress Cataloging-in-Publication Data
Spilsbury, Richard, 1963-
  Abstract expressionism / Richard Spilsbury.
      p. cm. -- (Art on the wall)
  Includes bibliographical references and index.
  ISBN 978-1-4329-1370-0 (hc)
  1. Abstract expressionism--United States--Juvenile literature. 2. Art, American--20th century--Juvenile literature. I. Title.
  N6512.5.A25S65 2008
  709.04'052--dc22

                              2008020361

Acknowledgments
The author and publisher are grateful to the following for permission to reproduce copyright material:
Alamy **pp. 32** (Michael Jenner), **36** (Arcaid); ARS, NY and DACS, London, U.K. 2008 **p. 28**; The Art Archive **p. 14** (Thyssen-Bornemisza Collection Madrid/The Willem de Kooning Foundation, New York/ARS, NY and DACS, 2008/Gianni Dagli Orti); Bridgeman Art Library **pp. 5** (Musée National d'Art Moderne, Centre Pompidou, Paris, France/DACS, London 2008/Lauros/Giraudon), **24** (Kate Rothko Prizel & Christopher Rothko ARS, NY and DACS, 2008/Purchased Through The Art Foundation of Victoria), **35** (Baselitz, Georg); Corbis **pp. 7** (Robert Holmes), **8** (Bettmann), **9** (Albright-Knox Art Gallery/DACS 2008/Estate of Arshile Gorky), **11** (Albright-Knox Art Gallery/Dedalus Foundation, Inc./VAGA, New York/ DACS 2008), **13** (Hans Hofmann/Burstein Collection), **18** (Francis G. Mayer), **23** (The Pollock-Krasner Foundation/ARS, NY and DACS, 2008), **27** (Helen Frankenthaler/Geoffrey Clements), **31** (Estate of Louise Nevelson/ARS, NY and DACS, London 2008), **37** (The Willem de Kooning Foundation); Chris Fairclough **pp. 20, 21**; Getty Images **pp. 17** (Martha Holmes/Time & Life Pictures), **19** (Photo by Fritz Goro/Time Life Pictures), **30** (Estate of David Smith/DACS, London/ VAGA, New York 2008/SHAUN CURRY/AFP), **33** (John Loengard/Time Life Pictures), **39** (Thomas S. England/Time Life Pictures); iStockPhoto **pp. 15, 22 bottom left** (Robert Churchill), **22 top right**, **22 bottom right**, **26, 29 & title page** (John Sigler), **38**; The Library of Congress, **p. 6**; National Archives and Records Administration **p. 10**.

Cover photograph: Hans Hofmann: *Summer* (1960) (Hans Hofmann/Burstein Collection/Corbis)

The Publishers would like to thank John Glaves-Smith for his invaluable help in the preparation of this book.

Contents

Some words are printed in bold, **like this**. You can find out what they mean by looking in the glossary.

What is Abstract Expressionism?

Many works of art are painted with careful, neat **brushstrokes** and show things that you can recognize, such as landscapes or groups of people. But the painting on page 5 consists mostly of rough lines and blotches. It looks as if the artist has painted wildly, in a terrible hurry to talk us through his image. It is one example of Abstract Expressionism.

The American movement

Abstract Expressionism is the name given to an important **movement** in art. It happened in the United States, especially in New York City. The movement lasted roughly from the mid-1940s to the early 1960s and, during this time, it was probably the most up-to-date and experimental, or **avant-garde**, American art. Abstract Expressionism became popular in Europe, too, and the United States became a major world center of art.

A movement in art can be when many artists paint in a similar style. For example, Pointillism was an art movement in Paris from the 1880s, when artists such as Paul Signac painted pictures made up of dots of paint. However, Abstract Expressionism is an art movement that includes a very wide variety of painting styles: for example, splatters and pools of paint produced by Jackson Pollock, distorted people created in bold, colorful brushstrokes by Willem de Kooning, and large panels of just one or two colors by Mark Rothko. What made Abstract Expressionist artists similar to each other was their ideas about art.

Spatter-and-daub

The term *Abstract Expressionism* was used to describe art quite a long time before Pollock and Rothko. In 1919, and in 1929, it was used to describe several paintings by artists including Wassily Kandinsky, a Russian avant-garde painter. However, it was in 1946 that the term was used for an art movement involving a group of artists. Art critic Robert Coates was describing paintings by Hans Hofmann, which he said were *"what some people have called the spatter-and-daub school of painting and I, more politely, have called Abstract Expressionism."*

Jackson Pollock created *Silver over Black, White, Yellow and Red* in 1948. He made it by pouring, splashing, and dribbling paint onto canvas.

Features of Abstract Expressionist art

In general, these four main things distinguish the work of Abstract Expressionist artists:

- The artists generally made their paintings and sometimes sculptures large, so the images dominate the viewer.
- They often applied paint with expressive marks, such as blobs of paint and coarse brushstrokes, which are a record of the artist at work.
- They felt that images carry a more powerful message if subjects are represented indirectly, rather than if things look real.
- Many of the artists hoped to show, or express, powerful feelings in their art, which people could relate to. Rothko said: *"I'm interested only in expressing basic human emotions—tragedy, ecstasy, doom, and so on."*

Art in the 1930s

In the 1930s, life was tough for many people. City employees lost their jobs and farmers' fields turned to dust. Tension between European countries was growing in the buildup to World War II. As in all periods of history, artists reacted to and depicted the changing times.

Depression

The 1920s had been boom years in many industrialized countries such as the United States, but this came to an end in 1929. The **Wall Street Crash**—when the U.S. stock market collapsed—was a huge blow. American banks went out of business, and countries in Europe were affected, too, because the United States suddenly reclaimed vast amounts of money that it had loaned to them in the boom time. By the early 1930s, the United States and much of Europe were in the depths of the **Depression**, a severe economic slump. Millions of people were left unemployed. Many were homeless and some even starved. The situation was made even worse in the United States by **drought** in farming regions. The drought turned fields where crops grew into barren, dusty plains.

Art during the Depression

One American art movement during the Depression was **Regionalism**. Regionalist artists worked in different styles, but they all wanted to show what life was like in the American countryside. Grant Wood in Iowa and Thomas Benton in Missouri painted portraits of real people and scenes of farming and country celebrations.

Many families in the crop-growing states, such as Oklahoma, had to abandon their land in the 1930s, when the rich soil turned to dust because of the drought.

John Curry in Kansas showed how tough life was for poor, rural folk, by showing their struggles during the drought. Curry's art was a comment on how the government was ignoring people's needs during the Depression.

The New Deal

In 1932, a new government was elected, led by President Franklin D. Roosevelt. It halted the Depression by making many changes to help people, called the **New Deal**. It loaned people money for food, houses, and land, and for farmers to grow crops. It set up schemes, such as the Works Progress Administration (WPA), to create jobs for people, including artists. The government created 5,000 jobs for artists,

Good for art?

Grant Wood argued that the Depression was good for American art, since it forced artists to focus on subjects in their own personal traditions and folklore, rather than looking further afield for inspiration. Regionalists believed that, after the Wall Street Crash, the big cities lost their attraction as places to get rich and prosper. Rural America was where most people lived and worked, and so this was where art should come from, too.

who produced over 200,000 works of art, including murals, or wall paintings, in hospitals, schools, and post offices.

This is part of a mural called *City Life*, painted in the 1930s inside the Coit Tower, San Francisco. The artist, Victor Arnautoff, was working for the Federal Art Project of the Works Progress Administration.

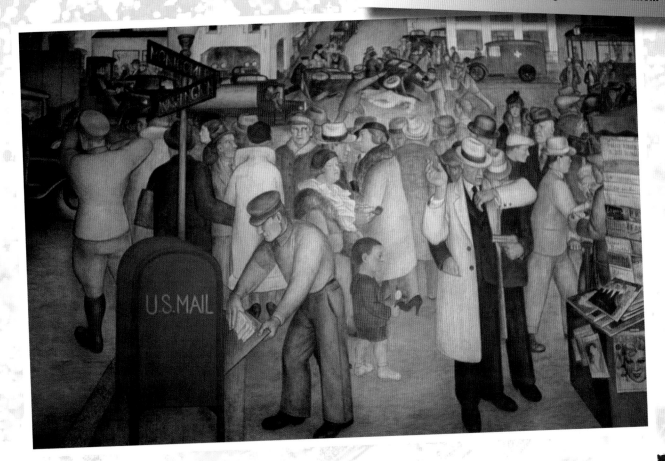

European directions in art

In Europe in the 1930s, there were two opposing directions in modern art. Some artists produced **abstract** art. Abstract art is nonrepresentational—it does not show objects, figures, and landscapes accurately, and its subjects are often unrecognizable. Instead, it uses lines, shapes, and colors to represent subjects or ideas. Some famous abstract painters of the time were Piet Mondrian and Wassily Kandinsky.

Other European artists belonged to a movement called **Surrealism**. Surrealist artists, such as Max Ernst, Salvador Dalí, and Joan Miró, painted pictures in which people and objects merge together, as if in a dream. The paintings were of images from inside their minds, and so revealed their emotions, fears, and fantasies.

From Europe to the United States

People from Europe had been migrating to the United States since the beginning of the twentieth century. Some hoped to get rich in a land of opportunity; others fled from Europe as refugees, to escape **persecution** in their own country. (*Persecution* means anything from being insulted or threatened, to being actually harmed.) Just before and during World War II, there was a sharp rise in the number of refugees, many of whom were Jews escaping **Nazi** persecution and people fleeing Nazi-occupied territories. Artist refugees who arrived in the United States included Mondrian, Ernst, Dalí, and Miró.

The German-born artist, Max Ernst (center), arrives in New York in 1941. He was one of many refugees escaping Nazi persecution.

Xhorkom-Summer, painted by Arshile Gorky in 1936, was named after Gorky's home town in Armenia. The central shape is said to be a heart.

New influences on American art

Exhibitions in the 1930s at the Museum of Modern Art in New York featured abstract and Surrealist European art. Some of the work shown was by immigrants, including Arshile Gorky and Marcel Duchamp, and some was by U.S. artists such as Arthur Dove. However, other influences on American artists at this time included the subjects and symbols used in ancient American art, such as on decorated pots created around 500 BCE by the Nazcas in Peru. Also, there was great interest in the modern public murals by the Mexican artist Diego Rivera, because of their large size and political subjects.

The first Abstract Expressionist?

Arshile Gorky was a very important link between European and new American painting styles in the 1940s. Some people even say that he was the first Abstract Expressionist artist. Gorky moved to the United States in 1920, to escape persecution by Turks in his native Armenia. He learned how to paint by copying artists, especially the abstract painter, Kandinsky, and the Surrealist, Miró.

The New York School

In the mid-1940s, several artists working in and around New York shared the idea of expressing their strong emotions through their art. This was a product of their feelings about the world just after World War II, and the belief that art should mirror the times. It was the start of a new movement that would place New York at the center of the art world.

Changing directions in art

Regionalist art had lost its popularity in the art world of New York by the start of the 1940s. People in the city associated Regionalism with the past, whereas the freedom of expression of abstract and Surrealist art represented modernity. However, events in Europe and Asia were having the most impact at this time. The United States had not been directly involved in the early part of World War II, but prospered from it, for example, by selling weapons. But after Japanese warplanes attacked U.S. Navy ships at Pearl Harbor in 1941, the United States joined the war. Thousands of U.S. troops left home for Europe and Asia. The American public then began to see shocking images and descriptions of suffering, death, and destruction, which were sent home by photographers, filmmakers, and journalists.

After the war, several young artists in New York felt that it was time for a new direction in art. They included Jackson Pollock, Franz Kline, Robert Motherwell, Ad Reinhardt, Mark Rothko, Barnett Newman, and Willem de Kooning. The artists all knew each other, but they did not work as a group or set out to form a movement in art. They felt that the world had revealed itself to be a more horrific place than before the war, for example, since atomic bombs had been dropped on Japan.

At the end of World War II, people saw the phenomenal power and destructive capabilities of atomic bombs for the first time. The mushroom-shaped cloud became a symbol of a new age.

Newman said:
"The war… has robbed us of our hidden terror, as terror can only exist if the forces of tragedy are unknown. We now know the terror to expect."

The artists wanted to express their feelings about the world directly through their work. They wanted to release their true, hidden emotions, just as the Surrealists did. Almost all of them were purely abstract artists, but they did not like the considered, unemotional work of geometric abstract painters such as Mondrian. They preferred art that showed the maker's gesture in making it. The artists were known at first as the **New York School**, and only later as Abstract Expressionists.

Robert Motherwell painted *Elegy to the Spanish Republic* in 1953 to express his feelings about the horrors of the Spanish Civil War in the 1930s. The dark shapes in the foreground may represent the forces of evil. The colors in the background are those of the Spanish flag.

Pollock said: *"It seems to me that the modern painter cannot express his age, the airplane, the atom bomb, the radio, in the old forms of the Renaissance or any past culture. Each age finds its own technique."*

Expressionism

The term *Abstract Expressionism* grew in part from an art movement called Expressionism, which emerged around the start of the twentieth century in Europe. Painters such as Vincent van Gogh, Edvard Munch, and Emil Nolde began to distort and exaggerate their subjects in order to increase the emotional impact on the viewer. They usually created paintings with rough brushstrokes and bright, unnatural colors.

Being universal

Earlier abstract artists had hoped to find a universal language of colors and shapes, which would mean something to everyone. For example, a contemporary of Mondrian said: *"The square is to us as the cross was to the early Christians."* Abstract Expressionist artists did not believe in this universal language, but they did believe in universal emotions, such as outrage, sorrow, and joy. They hoped to bring out these universal emotions by communicating them powerfully through their art.

The peak of painting

The influential American art critic, Clement Greenberg, thought that, in modern society, real or advanced art would become less and less appreciated by the public, who were interested mostly in popular culture. Therefore, advanced art would become cut off from the everyday world. The top artists would be experts purely in manipulating paint on canvas to the greatest effect, regardless of their subject and their emotional state when painting. Greenberg considered Abstract Expressionist painters, such as Rothko and especially Pollock, to be the greatest of their generation.

Why New York?

Abstract Expressionism started in New York and was the first U.S. art movement to become internationally famous. Since the artists were working in New York, the city became the center of trading in modern art. There were many rich people there who would buy new art, including members of the Guggenheim family. New art galleries opened to show off the new style, alongside expensive and highly appreciated works by artists such as Pablo Picasso and Fernand Léger. One of the new galleries, run by Peggy Guggenheim, was called The Art of This Century.

Spreading the word

Abstract Expressionist artists such as Pollock had originally moved to New York because it was the cultural capital city of the United States, where avant-garde culture from art to music could be experienced and learned about. New York was, and still is, a publishing center of the United States. Newspapers and magazines, such as *Time,* ran articles about the new art, which were distributed across the country. The new art form even appeared in mainstream magazines such as *Vogue,* which included photographs of models in front of Jackson Pollock paintings.

The art school

From the 1930s to the 1940s, many private art schools started in New York. Some were run by European artists who had had direct contact with artists such as Henri Matisse. Jackson Pollock studied at Hans Hofmann's art school. Hofmann was described by Greenberg as *"the most important art teacher of our time."* He taught a style of highly colored art that combined Expressionism and abstract art.

Summer (1960) shows how Hans Hofmann combined geometric shapes of abstract art and expressive paint marks. This approach inspired many of the younger Abstract Expressionists.

Willem de Kooning's *Abstraction* (1949) uses biomorphic shapes, which are typical of paintings from the early years of Abstract Expressionism.

suggest figures, objects, and landscapes. For example, can you see shapes a little like floating human figures, and even a face, in the painting by de Kooning shown above?

The early phase of Abstract Expressionism

The Abstract Expressionism that developed in New York can be divided into two broad phases. In the first, around the mid-1940s, artists such as Willem de Kooning, Arshile Gorky, and even Jackson Pollock, painted **biomorphic** shapes on their canvases. Biomorphic shapes are not realistic but look almost natural, as if they have grown and developed. With their free-form, nongeometric curves, the shapes often

The later phase

The later phase of Abstract Expressionism, throughout the 1950s, is divided into two very different styles. Some painters, such as Pollock and de Kooning, applied paint roughly, with great personal expression. They were less concerned with revealing the subject of the painting and more with the act of creating it. These paintings are often called **action paintings**. Many people think of this kind of work as being typical Abstract Expressionist art.

Other artists, however, such as Mark Rothko and Barnett Newman, created carefully painted, intense patterns of few colors. Abstract Expressionist works of this type are generally called **color-field paintings**.

Other action painters

At the same time as Abstract Expressionism flourished, similar art movements developed in Europe and Asia. Tachism, based in Paris, got its name from the French word for stain or spot. Tachists, such as Hans Hartung, Jean Dubuffet, and Nicolas de Stael, dripped, blotted, and stained paint into canvas. The Gutai group in Japan included artists such as Jiro Yoshihara and Murakami Saburo. Saburo is known for creating images by throwing an ink-stained ball at paper. Tachism and Gutai did not influence Abstract Expressionism directly, but all three movements were reactions to prewar abstract art.

Action painters

In 1952, the art critic, Harold Rosenberg, introduced the term *action painter* in the title of an article about Abstract Expressionists called "The American Action Painters." In the article, he wrote: *"At a certain moment, the canvas began to appear to one American painter after another as an arena in which to act... What was to go on the canvas was not a picture, but an event."*

Taking Action

Jackson Pollock laid a blank canvas on the floor. He watched how, by dribbling and pouring paint, a web of paint built up to create an image. He could control where the paint went, yet the painting became a record of his movements and revealed a little of how he was feeling when he made it. This is action painting. Other action painters, such as Franz Kline and Adolph Gottlieb, applied paint in different ways from Pollock, but all made the act of painting a vital part of their art.

Off the easel

For centuries, there had been a fairly standard way to paint on canvas. Artists would make a rectangular wooden frame and stretch canvas cloth across it. They used nails to hold the canvas tight, so that it was flat to paint on, and stood the canvas vertically on an easel. They would often coat the canvas with a thin paint called **primer**. When it has dried, the primer stops expensive colored paints from soaking into the cloth.

With the primed canvas on an easel, the artist might sketch a design on it. Then he or she would mix and blend paints on a palette, to make the colors wanted, and carefully apply them using brushes.

Pollock developed his distinctive style of painting in 1946–47, when he was looking for a new direction in his art. He chose to work off the easel. Instead, he nailed big, unstretched, and often **unprimed** canvases, or occasionally pieces of board, to the floor of his studio. Working on a

Pollock's influences

Several influences inspired Pollock's new style of painting. In the 1930s, he had encountered the technique and effect of drips and dribbles on easel paintings when he was studying art with other artists, including David Siqueiros, a Mexican mural painter. However, the biggest influence on Pollock was the sand paintings of Native Americans, such as the Navajo people. He had seen these being made when he lived in Arizona as a child. The paintings are generally made only during ceremonies held when people are sick. A medicine man, or tribal healer, carefully sprinkles different colors of sand onto the ground or cloths. The subjects formed from the sand include healing spirits, who are thought to have the power to make the sick person better.

Jackson Pollock at work in his Long Island, New York, studio. Pollock was very careful where he dribbled paint. Even though he controlled the painting process, he did not try to get rid of the random squiggles and splash marks of paint where it accidentally landed on his canvases.

horizontal surface instead of a vertical one meant that Pollock could move around the canvas to apply paint, and he could view the composition from all sides equally as he worked.

Brush-free

Pollock did not apply his paint in the traditional manner. He dribbled and flicked paint from the ends of old brushes, without touching the canvas. He poured paint from cans, forming glistening pools, and smeared or scratched it with sticks. His approach was not random. In 1950, he said: *"I can control the flow of paint: there is no accident."* There are curved and straight marks, and thin and thick lines in his work. The patterns look as if they were applied with rhythmic sweeps of his arms. Painting like this is often called **gestural**, because the particular gestures or movements that the artist used when painting have left their mark on the canvas.

Hidden under paint

Pollock expressed himself through hundreds of lines of paint, built up in layers. He often used enamel and aluminum paint, both of the types used for painting cars, because they were shiny. The gaps between the lines of paint that he dribbled and poured sometimes revealed parts of the canvas beneath, or colors that were added earlier. Sometimes they even revealed bits of older pictures, because Pollock recycled canvases on which he had already painted.

He sometimes added extra texture to the paint by mixing it with sand or objects including keys, buttons, cigarettes, and nails. *Blue Poles* is a composition with a black and green background overlaid with white, orange, and light gray marks and vertical dark blue "poles" applied with the straight edge of a piece of wood. The paint is studded with shards of broken glass. The shards are all that remains of large glass syringes that Pollock experimented with, to squeeze paint onto the canvas. The layers of paint and other materials on this and several others of Pollock's works are an inch or so thick.

The *New York Times* art critic, Howard Devree, compared the built-up paint on Pollock's paintings to "baked macaroni"!

Different action

Not all action painters worked like Pollock. In the early 1950s, Willem de Kooning, Philip Guston, and Franz Kline all used gestural brushstrokes to express themselves on canvas, and painted on easels. However, each had their own personal style which was something like a "signature."

De Kooning's subjects were always biomorphic and sometimes he even painted recognizable women, when most other Abstract Expressionist artists were making very abstract images. However, whatever his subjects, De Kooning always painted, reworked, and reworked again, tangled compositions with thick smears of paint.

Guston developed a way of painting using just vertical and horizontal overlapping brushstrokes. Toward the center of these paintings, such as *For M*, the brushstrokes get thicker and the tones of color get darker. Some critics called Guston's style "Abstract Impressionism." This was because the style recalled the work of **Impressionist** artists, such as Claude Monet (1840–1926), who painted the effects of changing natural light on landscapes.

Using the phone book

Franz Kline was a slow painter! He often spent many weeks or months on a picture, even though the finished compositions look as if they were painted quickly and spontaneously. This is because they were based on rapid ink sketches. Kline made so many sketches that it was too expensive to use proper art paper for them. So he sketched on old phone books, newspapers, and anything else he could find.

19

Try it yourself

Action!

Jackson Pollock said: *"When I am in my painting, I'm not aware of what I'm doing. It is only after a sort of get-acquainted period that I see what I have been about. I have no fears about making changes, destroying the image, etc., because the painting has a life of its own."* **Remember these words as you paint in the style of Pollock—using marbles!**

What you will need:

Different colored paints, such as poster paints

Old teaspoons

Bowls or empty pots

Sheets of paper

A flat box, large enough to hold the paper

Spherical glass marbles

Masking tape

1 **Tape a piece of paper flat inside the box.**

2 **Pour each color of paint you want to use into a separate bowl. Put two or three marbles in each bowl and roll them around to coat them with paint.**

3 **Half-fill another bowl with water, ready to clean off the paint-covered marbles before the paint dries on.**

4 **Use spoons to lift one or several marbles out of one of the bowls of paint and splat them onto the paper in the box.**

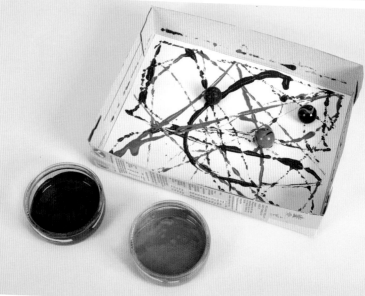

5   Roll the marbles around the box so that they create tracks. See how multiple marbles tend to leave parallel tracks, and how marbles can drag or even change direction when they cross over marble trails.

6   When you are happy with the trails from the first color, you can put the marble or marbles back in its bowl. Introduce a second, third, fourth, or however many colors you want, in the same way.

7   It's up to you when your painting is complete. Some people prefer more unpainted, white space between their trails. Pollock described this space as *"that which is left unsaid."*

8   Now make more paintings using the same technique.

Variations

- Leave all the marbles you use in the box, so that they are constantly mixing colors and making extra trails.
- Dribble and/or pour paint from spoons onto the paper.
- Paint on different types of paper, such as colored, textured, and absorbent.
- Use different kinds of paint, for example, some gloss and some matt.
- Sprinkle on glitter, sawdust, or sand to add texture to the paint.
- Use balls with different textures and sizes. For example, wrap lots of rubber bands around marbles or try golf balls.

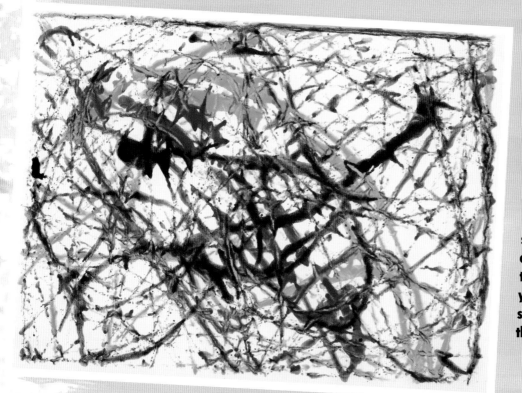

The next step
People who like Pollock's paintings say that they are something more than just trails of paint because the paints were applied with intensity, in response to deep feelings. Think of a movie or book that has made you feel happy, angry, relaxed, or sad. Then try the painting exercise again. If you did this exercise in a group, do you think you could guess someone's emotions from their painting?

Symbolic art

The action painter, Adolph Gottlieb, was interested in the idea that some **symbols** can be universally understood (see page 12), but he preferred to make up his own symbols rather than use existing ones. He painted a series called *Pictographs* in the 1940s. Each painting was divided into rough compartments, some with a symbol inside and others empty. Viewers might find meaning in the pictures if "reading" the symbols made them feel some emotion. However, since the symbols were essentially meaningless, other viewers might see Gottlieb's paintings as patterns of squiggles!

Try it yourself

Symbols
The symbols we see during our lives have many different meanings, from instructions to ideas. For example, a road sign with a horizontal white bar on a red circle means "Do not enter"; and the tao or yin-yang (below) is an ancient Chinese symbol representing harmony between different things. Choose a symbol that is important to you and make a beautiful painting of it.

Some Abstract Expressionist artists were inspired by the gestural marks used in the characters painted by Chinese calligraphers.

Gottlieb moved on to other series during the 1950s. For example, paintings in his *Burst* series each had a circular or ovoid object a little like the Sun at the top, and a broken, roughly painted form below, which looked as if it was exploding. This series, like *Pictographs*, was symbolic, but very mysterious in meaning.

Cut up

Some Abstract Expressionists experimented with **collage**. Collage is a composition made from cut or torn pieces of paper, canvas, or other materials, sometimes showing images, sometimes combined with paint. Lee Krasner developed her particular style of collage accidentally. One night she dropped a lot of her paintings, which she had not been able to sell, on the floor of her studio. The next morning she looked at the pattern they made and liked it so much that she cut up the canvases and stuck the pieces onto a sheet of material!

Conrad Marca-Relli happened on his collage technique, too. He wanted to depict white buildings in sunny Mexico, and realized that he could show the hard edges of buildings and their form by cutting up pieces of slightly different-colored light canvas. He then started to prepare abstract collages of material, which he overpainted with gestural brushstrokes.

Lee Krasner made her *Bald Eagle* collage in 1955.

Fields of Color

You can't take your eyes off the painting. It seems to radiate light from within the blocks of rich color soaked into its surface. The intense glow forces you to be quiet and think. This color-field painting is the work of Mark Rothko. Like other color-field painters, Rothko thought that to communicate meaning in his work was much more important than the act of creating it.

Contemplation

Color-field painting gets its name from the areas of just a few colors used in typical works. Color-field artists wanted to create art from within themselves, which would make viewers stop and contemplate, thinking deeply about the picture, themselves, and the world.

Rothko and Barnett Newman saw parallels between their art and religious art. In a Christian cathedral or Buddhist temple, images of Christ or the Buddha, and scenes from their lives, can lead worshipers to contemplate religious ideas. The artists believed that their paintings should have a similar effect.

The colored shapes seem to float and glow on this typical Mark Rothko color-field painting, called *No 37 (Red)*, from 1956.

The right place

Rothko was anxious that his works should be shown in a calm environment, for viewers to get the most out of them. The Rothko Chapel, Houston, Texas, was built to show his paintings. It is a place of contemplation for people of different faiths and art lovers.

In some art galleries, Rothko turned down the lighting so that his paintings could be seen in dim light, the same as in a church. Sometimes he insisted that galleries should restrict the numbers of visitors and put in benches for viewers' comfort. He once agreed to paint a set of pictures for a restaurant, but then gave the paintings to an art museum, because the mood of the restaurant would not have been right for viewing them.

Rothko said: *"The people who weep before my pictures are having the same religious experience I had when I painted them."* Newman said: *"Instead of making cathedrals out of Christ, man, or 'life,' we are making it out of ourselves."*

Color experience

In Rothko's paintings from the early 1950s onward, there are generally one, two, or three horizontal rectangles of different colors. Typical colors in his paintings of the early 1950s include red, yellow, and orange, but in the 1960s, his colors became darker, with more black, dark blues, and grays. The color fields are often arranged one above the other, against a plain colored background.

Ad Reinhardt's paintings from the 1950s are exclusively different shades of red or blue. Lots of small, colored rectangles overlap each other, so that some look as if they are in the background and others in the foreground.

Try it yourself

Contrast
Rothko and other color-field painters tried using contrasting colors next to each other to produce awe-inspiring visual effects. For example, orange looks more yellow next to red, and red looks redder next to blue. Visit http://webexhibits.org/colorart/contrast.html and near the bottom you can operate the contrast tool. See for yourself how five colors look very different against different colored backgrounds.

Think big

Rothko, Newman, and other artists helped people to experience the power of their paintings by making them very big. Most are over 7 feet (2 meters) high. Rothko suggested that painters of the past painted big to be "pompous," but that he had other reasons. He said it was: "... *precisely because I want to be very intimate and human. To paint a small picture is to place yourself outside your experience... However you paint the larger picture, you are in it.*" He even suggested viewers position themselves exactly 18 inches (45 centimeters) away from his paintings to get the best effect.

Soaking in

Rothko had a different painting approach from the action artists. Whereas Pollock built up gestural textures of paint on top of the canvas, Rothko let the paint soak into it. He usually worked at an easel.

To create a color field, Rothko first brushed a thin wash of intense color, in the shape he wanted, on an unprimed canvas. When this had soaked in, he added several layers of even thinner oil paint, in slightly different colors, over the top. He used fast, light brushstrokes. The layers overlapped, but the variable brushstrokes left some areas with deeper color than others. The edges of the rectangles were not solid lines but quite rough. Building up thin layers made the color fields more intense and even appear to hover above the background. Sometimes Rothko added egg to his paint to make it more luminous (light-reflecting). This was a technique used by medieval and Renaissance painters, too.

Try it yourself

Color depth
Here's one way to make vibrant colors in the style of Mark Rothko.

Take a large sheet of thick white paper. Mix a little dark red watercolor paint with lots of water, and brush the wash over the whole sheet.

Let it dry a little, but while it is still damp, paint two rectangular shapes, one above the other, in dark red watercolor. Together, they should almost fill the sheet. The paint should soak into the paper.

When the painting has dried completely, use the same red paint mixed with a small drop of white paint and a little water, to paint a slightly smaller rectangle on top of one of the first rectangles. Let it dry.

Finally, mix just a tiny bit of the red paint with water-based varnish, and brush a layer of this over the same rectangle. Does the color of one rectangle look deeper than that of the other?

Watery impressions

Helen Frankenthaler developed an unusual technique for making her color fields. She was inspired by Pollock to pour paint on canvases. However, the paint she used was very, very thin. She said: *"I didn't want to take a stick and dip it in a can of enamel. I needed something more liquid, watery, thinner. All my life, I have been drawn to water and translucency."* Frankenthaler mixed oil paint with liquids such as turpentine, to make it thin, and then rubbed it into the canvas, using sponges to stain the fabric.

Helen Frankenthaler poured on thin blue paint, which soaked into and stained the canvas. She added more thinner, so the blue varied from dark to light. The watery shape produced suggested the name for the painting, *The Bay* (1963).

Zips

Barnett Newman made vertical color fields on his canvases, instead of horizontal ones like Rothko. He generally painted one color over the entire canvas and then divided it into sections with one or several top-to-bottom lines. Newman called these lines "zips," because they suggested openings between the color panels that might reveal something underneath. He sometimes painted the zips freehand, without any guides, but usually he stuck on lines of masking tape and carefully painted over them.

This very stark zip painting by Barnett Newman, from 1958, is one of a series of paintings called *Stations of the Cross*. The title refers to the crucifixion (death on a cross) of Jesus, in Christian belief, even though the image does not look like a cross. Newman believed that the suffering of Jesus on the cross, caused by other people, had significance for everyone who had suffered during World War II, regardless of their religion or race.

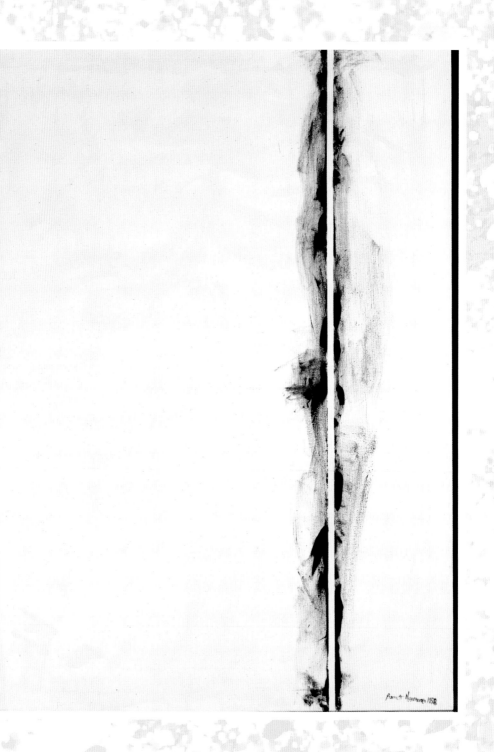

In the late 1950s, Newman took a slightly different approach. He stuck tape on white canvases, painted roughly over the tape, and then removed it. This left frayed-looking zips of brushstrokes around a neat line where the tape had stopped the paint from getting on the canvas.

Revealing details

Clyfford Still created color-field paintings that look rather like details of something much bigger extending beyond the edges of the canvas. Unlike Newman and Rothko, who poured, dribbled, or brushed on thin paint, Still used **palette knives** to smear on thick paint, right up to the edges of the canvas. You can often see the marks where the knife has scratched through the paint to the canvas beneath, and jagged gaps in one field reveal patches of different colors. The paintings look as if some colors were applied before others, and colors have been exposed by ripping off or wearing away a covering layer.

Parts of a whole

Clyfford Still considered each of his paintings as part of a whole, a little like snippets of a piece of music or pages from a diary. He said: *"To be stopped by a frame's edge is intolerable."* The titles of his paintings always consisted of just a number and a date.

He cared about the whole collection so much that he was reluctant to sell his works and lend them for exhibitions. In his will, he made sure that 90 percent of all the paintings he had ever made would stay together, and gave them to the city of Denver. In 2010, the city will open its Clyfford Still Museum to show his work.

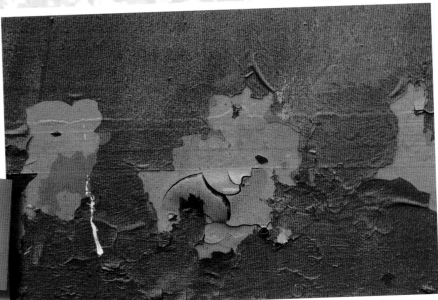

Clyfford Still's paintings can look a little like close-ups of old painted ships or doors, where chips of paint have come off, revealing paints used in the past.

Sculpture Expressions

The most likely place to see Abstract Expressionist art is on a wall. In the 1950s, people mostly wanted to buy paintings for their homes, galleries, and museums. But several American artists in the period after World War II expressed themselves through Abstract Expressionist sculptures.

Metal expressions

David Smith started as a painter, but is best known for the massive steel sculptures he made by **welding** metal pieces together. *Welding* means using intense heat to melt the pieces of metal, so that they stick together when they cool. Some of Smith's sculptures are made from pieces of old plows and other tools found on the farm where he lived. Others are tall stacks of triangles, circles, rectangles, cylinders, and cuboids, constructed from metal.

Working metal takes much longer than painting, but Smith's sculptures still give the impression that he was expressing his feelings. The shapes are delicately balanced and look as if they have been arranged spontaneously, without lots of planning. Smith sometimes scratched the surfaces of his shiny metal sculptures with a wire brush. The marks are gestural and are a record of the artist at work, just like the dribbles of paint on a Pollock painting.

Photographers take pictures of David Smith's *Zig IV* (1961) at an exhibition of his work in London, England. This is a typical Smith sculpture made of welded, curved steel plates.

Assembling wood

Louise Nevelson made Abstract Expressionist sculptures from wooden objects she found in the street. In the 1940s, she started to nail together objects as varied as baseball bats, parts of staircases, driftwood, and offcuts of wood, often inside wooden crates. She then sprayed the whole piece with black paint to cover up variations in color and texture, and to make the work more mysterious.

Nevelson's inspiration to work with wood came partly from her past. Her Jewish family emigrated from Russia in 1905, to escape persecution, and settled in Maine. There, she started to notice the shadows and shapes made by stacks of wood at her father's new lumberyard. As an adult living in New York, Nevelson assembled wood shapes in her sculptures, partly to remind her of her family's past.

Try it yourself

Find a sculpture
Gather together waste you find at home, such as old CDs, used pens, worn-out video tapes, and yoghurt pots. Pack the objects closely together on a piece of thick cardboard or inside a shallow cardboard tray. The idea is to contrast different shapes and textures. Stick the objects in position using glue or adhesive paper tape and finally, paint or spray the whole piece with black, shiny, metallic paint.

The Decline of Abstract Expressionism

Movements in art come and go. Just as Abstract Expressionism became the most important movement in American art in the 1950s, so other movements such as **Pop Art** took over in the 1960s. Yet the work of Abstract Expressionist artists continues to be appreciated by art lovers in today's ever-changing world.

Changing tastes

It is tricky to say exactly when Abstract Expressionism started to decline. By the late 1950s, fewer new artists were becoming well-known for making expressive, gestural art. Some of the most famous Abstract Expressionist artists died at this time, including Jackson Pollock in 1956 and Franz Kline in 1962. By the early 1960s, even painters such as Mark Rothko and Willem de Kooning were finding it more difficult to show their new work, because galleries no longer considered them avant-garde.

The images on these bags for sale in a market in London are based on the comic strip-style paintings that were characteristic of the Pop artist, Roy Lichtenstein.

In 1962, the Sidney Janis Gallery in New York marked the changing tastes in art with an exhibition called *The New Realists*. This included work by young American artists, such as Andy Warhol and Roy Lichtenstein, who used images and styles from advertising posters and comics. They believed that the subjects used by Abstract Expressionists were too obscure for normal people to be able to relate to their work. The "new realist" work was, in fact, the beginning of Pop Art, which ruled the American art world for the rest of the 1960s. Pop artists wanted to make art that expressed nothing about themselves, but instead, showed the world around them.

Dead end

During the 1960s, color-field painting started to change. Some painters became less gestural and painted flatter, more geometric shapes. These shapes had very clearly defined edges, and so this style of art was called **Hard-Edge painting**. Painters in this style, such as Frank Stella and Ad Reinhardt, emphasized the picture as an object and no longer as a representation of a particular subject. Stella said a painting was *"a flat surface with paint on it—nothing more."* Many viewers could not appreciate Hard-Edge paintings as they could color-field art, and therefore, they felt that this direction in art had reached a dead end.

The last painting

Ad Reinhardt painted a series of square black canvases in the 1960s. If viewers spent some time looking at the canvases, they could see that the color was not uniform. Reinhardt's canvases were divided up into nine equal squares, some painted in matt and others in gloss black paint. The tone was the same, but the luminosity varied. He suggested that the black paintings reduced color to near invisibility, and therefore were *"the last painting anyone can hope or wish to paint."*

At work in his studio, Ad Reinhardt paints one of the black paintings. Reinhardt believed that these almost nonexistent images had the power to make people contemplate religion and other deep thoughts.

Less is more

The Hard-Edge paintings of Reinhardt and Stella, and their beliefs about abstract art, were important in the development in the 1960s of an art movement called **Minimalism**. Minimalist art is paintings or sculptures that are stripped down to their most essential features. Reinhardt said: *"The more stuff in it, the busier the work of art, the worse it is. More is less. Less is more."*

Most of the more famous Minimalists are from the United States. They include Richard Serra, who made giant sculptures from pieces of unaltered sheet steel, Sol LeWitt, who designed enormous wall drawings in pencil and chalk to be made directly on gallery walls, and Carl Andre.

Andre's *Equivalent VIII* or *The Bricks* is a famous Minimalist sculpture. It is simply a rectangular stack of 120 bricks. This piece from 1966 has made people question what art is. For example, in 1976, after the work was bought by the Tate Gallery in London, the journalist Keith Waterhouse wrote: *"Bricks are not works of art. Bricks are bricks. You can build walls with them… but you cannot stack them two deep and call it sculpture."*

Moving art

In the 1960s, New York galleries showed the work of many European artists who were interested in creating movement in their work. Painters, including Victor Vasarely from Hungary and Bridget Riley from Britain, painted stripes of colors and patterns on their canvases. These designs caused blurring or a sense of movement for people looking at the work. This type of art was called Optical or **Op Art**.

Other artists created sculptures with parts that actually moved. Julio Le Parc from Argentina used motors to move electric lights, and the Greek artist, Takis, used magnets to move needles. Art that uses actual movement to create its effect is called **Kinetic Art**.

Motion picture art

Len Lye was a New Zealand Kinetic artist who often worked with film. One of his first pieces, from the 1930s, was made by painting and scratching directly onto offcuts of film from a movie studio. He did this because he could not afford to shoot proper movies! Lye stuck the offcuts together and synchronized the movement on screen with rhythmic music. He used this approach to make many movies, up until his death in 1980.

Abstract Expressionism revisited

Abstract Expressionism has had a great influence on art created since the 1960s. For example, from the 1970s to 1980s, there was a worldwide movement called **Neo-Expressionism**, in which artists, including Georg Baselitz from Germany and Julian Schnabel from the United States, painted highly gestural, nonabstract art. Their approach was directly influenced by artists such as Hofmann, de Kooning, and Pollock. Neo-Expressionist artists, and later avant-garde artists, were also influenced by the way Abstract Expressionists took risks in creating new art styles to express themselves.

Georg Baselitz paints with as much gesture as many Abstract Expressionists did, but always represents recognizable subjects, as in *Double Portrait* (1987). However, his unusual approach is to almost always show his subjects upside down. This makes the paintings seem more abstract.

Abstract Expressionism for sale

People still buy Abstract Expressionist art today. They mainly buy reproductions on postcards, posters, prints, and calendars, when they visit art galleries and exhibitions. However, home furnishing stores also sell framed prints of work by Pollock and others, to complement the modern furniture and fittings they offer for twenty-first-century homes. The popularity of the art has been helped by major exhibitions at museums and galleries, from a **retrospective** of Clyfford Still at the Museum of Modern Art, New York, in 1979, to "Rothko at the Tate" in London, in 2008.

High interest from the public and from art collectors has made original Abstract Expressionist paintings some of the most expensive post-World War II art at auction. For example, in 2008, David Rockefeller sold *White Center (Yellow, Pink and Lavender on Rose)* by Rothko for $72.8 million. This was a staggering increase in value from when he bought the work from the artist in 1969, for $10,000!

The David and Peggy Rockefeller Gallery is part of the Museum of Modern Art (MoMA) in New York, one of the main places where Abstract Expressionist works of art can be seen.

The worth of the art has created interest from criminals. For example, a Pollock valued at over $11 million was stolen from a museum in Pennsylvania, in 2005.

The lasting appeal of Abstract Expressionism

Over 50 years after it first emerged in New York, Abstract Expressionist art still has widespread appeal. The Abstract Expressionists are important partly for the art they created. This abstract art has not dated. Its power and scale still cause awe and contemplation in the viewer. We can still imagine the energy and deep thought that must have helped the artists to create their work.

Many artists today, such as Fiona Rae in Britain, paint in very gestural ways and explore the significance of symbols in their work, just as action painters did in the past. The other reason why Abstract Expressionist artists continue to inspire others is that they took risks in following their own individual styles. This encourages artists of today to do the same and keep on "pushing the boundaries" of avant-garde art.

Willem de Kooning and his wife Elaine in their studio in 1985. They often worked together on paintings as they got older.

Survivors

The surviving Abstract Expressionist artists went in different directions through the 1960s, 1970s, and 1980s. Adolph Gottlieb continued working in the same style. Clyfford Still stopped painting, moved away from New York, and lived on his farm. Willem de Kooning created many sculptures and prints in the early 1970s, but then his work dried up because he became sick. However, in the 1980s, he painted hundreds of colorful, abstract works that some critics consider among his best.

Getting into Art

Do you feel inspired to splatter paint on canvas or to create big abstract paintings in rich panels of color? Have you ever wanted to express your feelings through art? If so, then maybe you should brush up on your art skills and learn more about different movements in art.

Build up your technique

Almost every abstract painter or sculptor learned how to draw first. So, get sketching everything and anything, from pets and curtains to still lives and landscapes! Think about how to depict different shapes and forms, colors, and textures. Experiment with different media, from pencil and charcoal to ink and paint. Try making paintings not only with brushes, but also using palette knives and sponges or by pouring and splattering colors. There is no right or wrong way to express yourself through art, so don't be afraid to use lots of paper as you build up your technique.

Study and inspiration

Once you know you are really serious about art, you will need to study. The obvious first step is to choose art as a study subject at school. However, art classes last only a few hours per week, so make more time for your art by joining lunchtime or after-school art clubs, or by attending classes at a local college, museum, or gallery. Your aim should be to try different styles and media

Try it yourself

Quick draw
Some Abstract Expressionist artists worked fast to get their ideas on paper or canvas. Practice sketching objects fast. Ask a friend or family member to collect some objects for you to draw—maybe an iron, cans, telephones, flowers, stones, or kitchen utensils.

Get a sketch pad and pencil, and when you are ready, ask the friend to show you each item on its own for just 30 seconds. You will struggle to complete a sketch within the time limit, especially at first, but you will soon learn how to draw different shapes quickly.

When sketching quickly, concentrate on the overall shape and proportions of objects rather than their fine detail.

until you find one that you feel comfortable with. The next step is going to art school. Here you will find a wider range of art opportunities and meet other people who are enthusiastic about art.

Through all this study you will need some inspiration. For that, head to art galleries and museums. You will be able to see examples of art from many different movements in art, including Abstract Expressionism. Pictures in books and on the Internet, movies, and TV programs all help to give an idea of paintings and sculptures, but seeing them for real lets you appreciate and contemplate the wonderful scope of textures, materials, colors, and size in completely different ways.

A future in art

With all those art qualifications, what comes next? Some people become artists, but others use their art degrees or diplomas to get other jobs. These include work in galleries or auction houses, deciding on values of art and helping to sell it to art collectors; and teaching, to pass on art skills to other people. Some art teachers work as art therapists, helping people to express themselves in art as a way of overcoming health difficulties.

Art therapy in action at a hospital. Painting to express feelings of frustration and pain can help people to cope better with an illness.

Lives of the Artists

Willem de Kooning (1904–97)

Willem de Kooning was born in Rotterdam, the Netherlands, where he studied commercial and fine art before emigrating to the United States in 1926. At first, he survived by painting and decorating, before becoming a painter after a year on the Works Progress Administration (WPA) Federal Art Project. In the early 1940s, he painted abstracts and figures, and later worked mainly in black and white. Works include *The Women* (early 1950s) and *Parkways*.

Lee Krasner (1908–84)

Born in Brooklyn, New York, Lee Krasner knew she wanted to be an artist from a young age. During the Depression, she worked during the day and attended art classes at night. After meeting and marrying Jackson Pollock, she further developed her own abstract style. She worked on color-field paintings and collages, sticking large dramatic shapes on canvas. After Pollock's sudden death, she expressed her loss in large gestural works such as *The Guardian* (1960). Other works include *Untitled* (1949) and *Gothic Landscape* (1961).

Helen Frankenthaler (born 1928)

Helen Frankenthaler was born in New York, where she trained in art and met Abstract Expressionist artists, such as Pollock, Krasner, and De Kooning. Frankenthaler extended Pollock's technique of dripping paint on a floor canvas by developing a method of staining untreated canvases and using thin washes of color. This method gave her paintings a distinctive floating effect. Works include *Mountains and Sea* (1952) and *Seven Types of Ambiguity* (1957).

Barnett Newman (1905–70)

A painter and sculptor, Barnett Newman was born in New York, where he studied and taught art. He developed his technique of painting fields of color separated by one or more vertical stripes that he called "zips" in the late 1940s. He went on to paint in black and white and make sculptures. Works include *Moment* (1946), *Eve* (1950), *Adam* (1951), and a series called *Eighteen Cantos* (1963–64).

Jackson Pollock (1912–56)

Jackson Pollock was a leading figure in the Abstract Expressionist art movement. Inspired by Native American sand painting and by Surrealism, he developed his own style of gestural painting, using his technique of dripping paint on a canvas on the floor. He married the painter Lee Krasner in 1944. In the early 1950s, he started to work in black and white, but his career was cut short when he died in a car crash. Famous works include *Summertime Number 9A* (1948), *Number 14* (1951), and *Yellow Islands* (1952).

Ad Reinhardt (1913–67)

Ad Reinhardt was born in New York, the son of Russian and German immigrants. He began to work in an abstract style in the 1930s, was a pioneer of Hard-Edge painting after the war, and became friendly with Abstract Expressionist artists. His paintings gradually became completely symmetrical, and in the 1950s, he began to work in a single color, moving from red to blue and then to his final stage of black. Works include *Abstract Painting* (1951–52), *Abstract Painting No.5* (1962), and *Abstract Painting* (1966).

David Smith (1906–65)

The American sculptor and painter, David Smith, was a friend of Abstract Expressionist painters but began to concentrate on sculpture in the 1930s. This started with attaching wood and other materials to his paintings, after which he made sculptures from iron or steel. He made bird sculptures and totem figures, often using found objects. From the early 1950s, his work became much larger and simpler. Works include *Agricola IX* (1952), *Forging XI* (1955), and *The Five Spring* (1956).

Mark Rothko (1903–70)

The painter Mark Rothko was born Marcus Rothkowicz in Russia and emigrated with his family to the United States in 1913. In 1923, he moved to New York, studied art, and then began to paint on his own. In the 1930s, his pictures already had flat areas of color. In the 1940s, he made Surrealist and biomorphic paintings, before adopting his famous Abstract Expressionist color-field paintings in 1947, works that gradually became darker. Works include *Light Red over Black* (1957), *Black on Maroon* (1958 and 1959), and *Red on Maroon* (1959).

Clyfford Still (1904–80)

In the 1930s, the American painter, Clyfford Still, began painting semi-abstract pictures with glimpses of figures or landscape. After World War II, he moved to New York and became friends with Abstract Expressionist artists such as Rothko and Pollock. He exhibited and taught for awhile, but then became more isolated, eventually detaching himself from the art world completely. His works include *Jamais* (1944) and *1948* (1948).

1915 Hans Hofmann opens his first art school in Munich, where he teaches Louise Nevelson.

1923 The Russian immigrant, Marcus Rothkowicz (later to change his name to Mark Rothko), moves to New York, where he paints and teaches art for the next 47 years.

1929 The U.S. stock market crashes on October 24, "Black Thursday," triggering a worldwide economic collapse—the Great Depression—which will last until the beginning of World War II.

The Museum of Modern Art, New York, opens. The American public and artists can now see a broad selection of twentieth-century European and American art.

Jackson Pollock begins studies in New York with Thomas Benton, a Regionalist artist.

1932 Franklin Delano Roosevelt is elected president of the United States and develops economic and social reforms, known as the New Deal, to help millions of Americans through the Depression.

The Empire State Building in New York is completed, although the Depression means that there is little demand for the offices inside.

1933 The Mexican muralist, Diego Rivera, is commissioned to create a mural in New York's Rockefeller Center. Rivera's work, along with that of his compatriots José Orozco and David Siqueiros, influences many American artists employed in government-sponsored New Deal projects.

Hofmann opens Hans Hofmann's School of Fine Arts in New York.

David Smith starts making welded steel sculptures.

1935 The U.S. government launches the Works Progress Administration (WPA), which provides employment for artists such as making murals, sculptures, and posters for public buildings and exhibitions.

Mark Rothko, Adolph Gottlieb, and others form an artists' group in New York called "The Ten," who all paint in an Expressionist style.

1937 Lee Krasner enters Hofmann's school.

1939 World War II begins when German troops invade Poland. France, Britain, and later Canada declare war against Germany.

1939 (cont.) John Steinbeck's novel *The Grapes of Wrath* is published, telling the story of a farming family from Oklahoma, displaced by the Dust Bowl.

Barnett Newman stops painting during the war.

1941 Following the bombing of Pearl Harbor by Japanese warplanes, the United States and Britain declare war on Japan.

Gottlieb begins his series of *Pictographs*.

1942 Peggy Guggenheim opens The Art of This Century gallery in New York.

1943 Pollock's first one-man exhibition takes place at The Art of This Century.

1944 Pollock marries Lee Krasner. Ad Reinhardt serves in the U.S. Navy.

1945 World War II ends when the United States drops atomic bombs on Hiroshima and Nagasaki, Japan.

1947 Pollock's action painting style emerges.

1948 Rothko moves from biomorphic abstract paintings to color-field paintings, using his recognizable style of soaked-in paint. Newman paints his first "zip" images.

1950 Newman's first one-man show is held at the Betty Parsons Gallery, New York.

1952 Helen Frankenthaler paints her influential *Mountains and Sea*.

1953 Krasner starts a series of Abstract Expressionist collages.

1956 Pollock dies in a car crash.

1961 Clyfford Still gives up painting.

1962 Andy Warhol paints *Campbell's Soup Cans*, a key work of the Pop Art movement.

Franz Kline dies.

1964 The term *Op Art* is coined in *Time* magazine to describe paintings and sculptures that make use of optical effects.

1965 David Smith dies in a truck accident.

1967 Retrospective of Pollock's paintings at the Museum of Modern Art, New York.

Ad Reinhardt dies.

Rothko finishes paintings specially made for a Rothko Chapel in Texas.

1970 Rothko and Newman die.

Glossary

abstract in art, including little that is recognizable or realistic, but being made up of shapes, colors, or lines

action painting style of Abstract Expressionism, where artists such as Pollock applied color with energy and bold movements to show their emotion when painting

avant-garde new and experimental. Abstract Expressionism was avant-garde in the 1940s and 1950s.

biomorphic drawn, painted, or sculpted with curved shapes, which are abstract and yet inspired by living things. Biomorphic shapes often remind us of real, natural objects such as trees or animals.

brushstroke mark left by a brush loaded with paint. Brushstrokes differ in terms of their direction, texture, and the thickness of the paint.

collage work of art that includes elements, often paper or material, that have been stuck onto another surface

color-field painting style of Abstract Expressionism, where artists, such as Rothko, applied rich color in large blocks

Depression period during the 1930s when there was a widespread economic decline. Businesses and banks failed, and there was mass unemployment, for example, in the United States and Germany.

drought period of time when there is insufficient rainfall for crops to grow and to supply other human or environmental needs

gestural describes art with obvious marks, such as brushstrokes or drips of paint, created with strong movement and intensity of feeling

Hard-Edge painting movement in art following Abstract Expressionism in the United States, where paintings were created with very few, plain, color fields. Hard-Edge painters included Ad Reinhardt and Frank Stella.

Impressionism movement in art from the late nineteenth century, when artists such as Claude Monet tried to paint the effect of light on colors, typically using small brushstrokes

Kinetic Art art movement in the middle of the twentieth century where artists used wind, magnets, motors, and other energy sources to make parts of their works move. For example, Alexander Calder made steel mobiles that twisted in the breeze. The effect of the movement in such works is to make their forms and colors vary.

Minimalism movement in art in the late 1960s, where artists such as Carl Andre used very few or minimal elements of the simplest possible form. They often used industrially produced elements such as bricks or sheet steel.

movement style or approach to art practiced by several artists in a particular period, and sometimes in a particular place. Abstract Expressionism was a movement that happened in the period after World War II, in New York.

Nazi member of the dominant political party in Germany from 1933 to 1945. The Nazi party promoted anti-Semitism, racism, nationalism, and militarism. The Nazis invaded parts of Europe, started World War II, and carried out the Holocaust, or systematic killing of millions of people.

Neo-Expressionism movement in art in the 1970s, where artists such as Georg Baselitz created vast, gestural but nonabstract paintings

New Deal President Roosevelt's 1932 agenda for change in the United States, designed to help people recover from the Depression

New York School the name that was first used for the group of Abstract Expressionist artists

Op Art art movement in the 1960s, where abstract artists painted lines and shapes to produce visual effects of movement for viewers. Op artists include Bridget Riley, who painted lines that appear to blur into one another.

palette knife wide, bent knife used to spread paint on canvas and other surfaces

persecution persistent ill-treatment or harassment of a person or group of people

Pop Art movement in art in the late 1950s to 1960s, largely in the United States, where artists such as Andy Warhol created images from popular, mass-produced culture, often using commercial art techniques

primer preparatory coating put on a surface before painting over the top. On canvas, primer helps to stop oil paint from soaking in.

Regionalism movement in art in the United States in the 1930s to 1940s, when artists such as Grant Wood chose traditional folk themes that celebrated small-town, and not urban, America

retrospective exhibition looking back at an artist's work and showing how it developed over a period of time

Surrealism movement in art from the 1920s to 1930s, in which artists, such as Salvador Dalí, made images based on their dreams and subconscious thoughts

symbol image or shape that represents something else. For example, a cross is a symbol of Christianity.

unprimed not treated with primer

Wall Street Crash event at the New York stock exchange, on Wall Street, on a single day in October 1929, when the value of many banks and businesses dropped. This caused many people in the United States and in other places to lose lots of money.

weld connect two pieces of a material, such as metal or plastic, by heating and melting together

Find Out More

Books

ART USA: The American Art Book (Mini Edition). New York: Phaidon, 2001.

Barnes, Rachel. *Abstract Expressionists* (Artists in Profile) Chicago, IL: Heinemann Library, 2002.

Bieringer, Kelley. *Is Modern Art Really Art?* (What Do You Think?). Chicago, IL: Heinemann Library, 2008.

Venezia, Mike. *Jackson Pollock* (Getting to Know the World's Greatest Artists). Danbury, CT: Children's Press, 1994.

Wills, Charles A. *America in the 1950s* (Decades of American History). New York: Chelsea House Publications, 2005.

Useful websites

Sites featuring individual artists

Jackson Pollock:
www.nga.gov/feature/pollock/index.htm

Mark Rothko:
www.nga.gov/feature/rothko/

Clyfford Still:
www.clyffordstill.net/

Louise Nevelson:
www.thejewishmuseum.org/site/pages/content/exhibitions/special/nevelson/nevelson_onlinefeature.html

Websites with things to do

www.jacksonpollock.org/
Here you can paint like Pollock online! Press on your left-hand mouse button, and start dribbling! Change color by pressing the mouse button again.

www.tate.org.uk/
Visit the Learn online section to listen to podcasts about various modern painters including Pollock, Rothko, and the Mexican muralist, Siqueiros.

Visit the Tate collection section and you can check out biographies and selected images of any of the artists mentioned in this book. There are also descriptions of art movements.

http://arts.guardian.co.uk/art/news/story/0,,2219685,00.html
A set of 32 paintings attributed to Jackson Pollock were discovered in 2005 in a storage locker. No one had ever seen them before. Are they real or fakes? Follow the leads starting at the website address above.

General sites on Abstract Expressionism and the history of modern art

www.tate.org.uk/
Visit the Tate collection section and you can check out biographies and selected images of any of the artists mentioned in this book. There are also descriptions of art movements.

www.metmuseum.org/toah/hm/11/hm11.htm
What types of art were being created around the world at the same time as Abstract Expressionism flowered in New York? The website of the Metropolitan Museum of Art in New York has a comprehensive timeline of Art History. You can click on different centuries on the timeline at the top, and then on different regions of the world map to find out more.

www.artlex.com/ArtLex/a/abstractexpr.html This is an online art dictionary. In the Index, click on A–Ac, and scroll down until you reach Abstract Expressionism. There is a short description of the movement and then lots of thumbnails of Abstract Expressionist works of art to look at.

Artists and movements to research

Why not extend your art studies by finding out more about other Abstract Expressionist artists and movements influenced by Abstract Expressionism? Use Google or any search engine on Internet Explorer, Netscape, or Mozilla to carry out your research.

Other American art movements:

Lyrical Abstraction

Mexican Muralists

American Scene Painting or Regionalism

Later Abstract Expressionists:

Cy Twombly

Joan Mitchell

Sam Francis

Abstract artists who were influenced by Abstract Expressionism:

German artists Anselm Kiefer and Gerhard Richter

Modern British artist Fiona Rae

Galleries

The following places have great selections of Abstract Expressionist art:

Tate Modern, London, England, U.K.

Metropolitan Museum of Art, New York

Museum of Modern Art, New York

Whitney Museum of American Art, New York

National Gallery of Australia, Canberra, Australia

Georges Pompidou Centre, Paris, France

Tehran Museum of Contemporary Art, Tehran, Iran

Index